Coming Together

By M.C. Hall

Scott Foresman
is an imprint of

Glenview, Illinois • Boston, Massachusetts • Chandler, Arizona •
Upper Saddle River, New Jersey

Photographs

Every effort has been made to secure permission and provide appropriate credit for photographic material. The publisher deeply regrets any omission and pledges to correct errors called to its attention in subsequent editions.

Unless otherwise acknowledged, all photographs are the property of Pearson Education, Inc.

Photo locators denoted as follows: Top (T), Center (C), Bottom (B), Left (L), Right (R), Background (Bkgd)

Opener: ©Image Source
1 Jupiter Images
3 ©Randy Faris/Corbis
5 ©Image Source
6 ©Tom & Dee Ann McCarthy/Corbis
8 Jupiter Images

ISBN 13: 978-0-328-46899-7
ISBN 10:   0-328-46899-1

7 8 9 10 V010 13

Did you ever move to a new place?
Everything seems different.
Then we meet new friends.
Our new friends may be different.
But soon we come together to do
many things.

We come together to learn.

We go to school.

We talk and read together.

We spend time getting to know each other.

We come together to have fun.

We swim and ride bikes.

We visit zoos and parks.

We have fun watching sports together.
Sometimes we clap for the same team.
Sometimes we clap for different teams!

We come together to help our towns. We pick up trash, and we plant flowers and trees.

We come together to help one another. We gather food and give the food to families who need it.